by Dorsey Craig

Copyright ©2007 by Dorsey Craig

All rights reserved. No part of this publication may be reproduced, stored in a retrieval system or transmitted in any form or by any means, electronic, mechanical, photocopying, recording or otherwise, without the prior written permission of the author.

ISBN 978-0-6151-4475-7

Published by Dorsey Craig
Design, layout, cover and illustrations by Dorsey Craig

Printed in the United States of America

Love what you do
Do what you love

Contents

Illuminate	*9*
Synergy	*11*
The Last Lunch	*13*
Focused Outlook	*15*
Thrive	*19*
Stain Release	*21*
Authentic Strive	*25*
Renewed Purpose	*27*
Amusement	*29*
Poised Perception	*31*
Anchor	*33*
Breathe	*35*
Direction	*37*
Maintain	*39*

Illuminate

Illuminate

If thrown off course
And begin to remorse
Start to rehearse
This simple verse
Remain like the palm
Peaceful and calm
Swaying with the wind
Resilient to the bend
Until one is able to stand again
With all the joy
Needed to glare at life as a toy
Wanting to play
Not as a stray
But as several rays
Shining upon
The glass that's spun
From the sands of time
While keeping in mind
The process of the grind
To refine and inline
Retrospective time
When life was a dime
Could only count to ten
Life was simply splendid then
To go out and play
Would even send hunger away
One must stay
In a state of clay
Able to accept
Whatever life may project
With self respect

Synergy

Synergy

No need to chew
To digest this stew
Cold pressed as a brew
Infused patiently through
Fermented edges
Converted into liquid ledges
Of spoken verb
Cemented in written word
The outlook of language in its ordinary everyday form
Resonating a pleasurable sensation streaming from
Communication not lingering in translation to long
Similar to the penetrating lyrics of a song
But without the assistance of music to sing along
That's where life will provide a melody to hum
While following the beat of the hearts drum

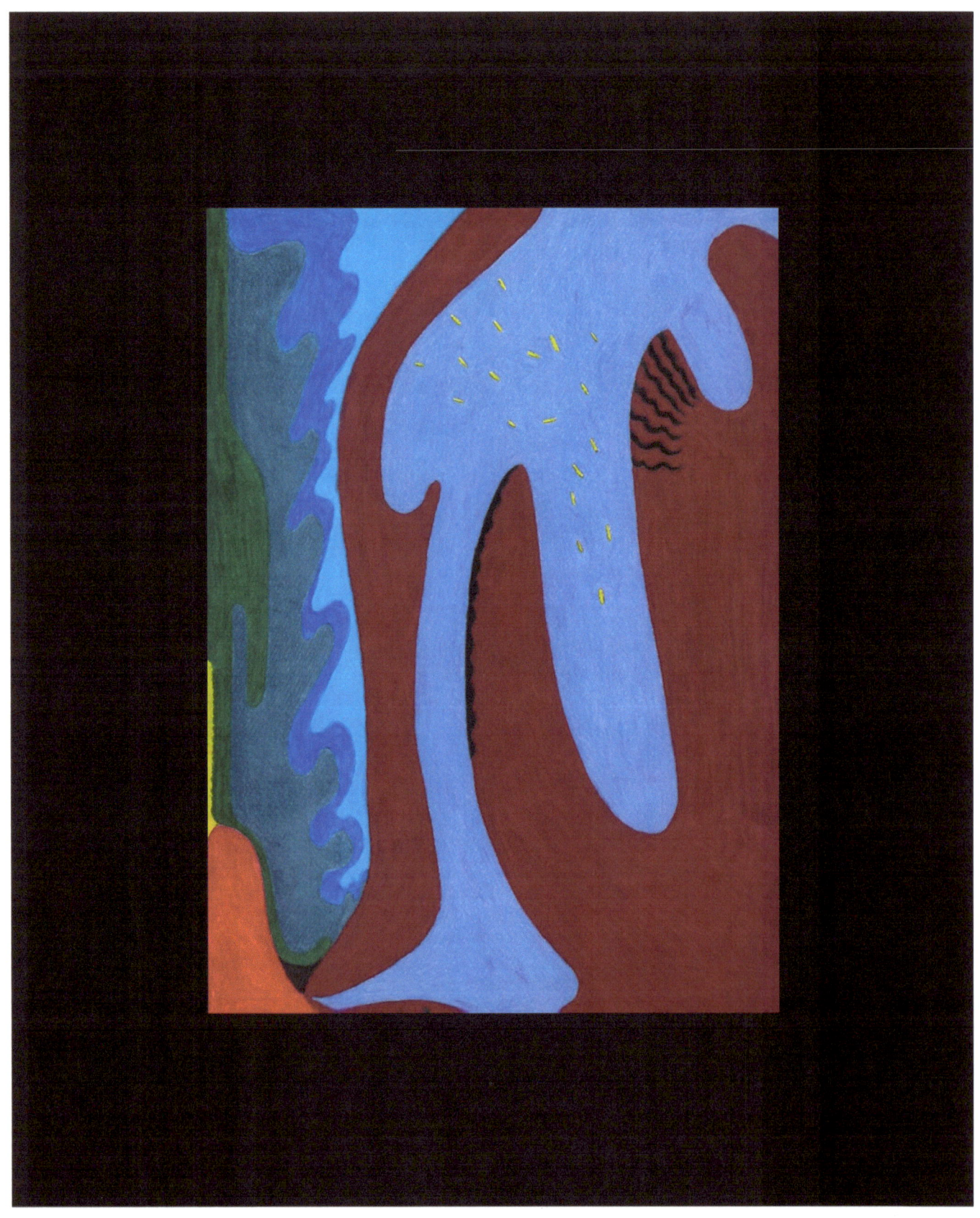

The Last Lunch

The Last Lunch

I decided to invite
My triplet brother out for a bite
It was quite nice
He had curry chicken and I fried rice
He wore a red button shirt
Also red shorts
That cut just above the knee
While sporting a fresh cut goatee
I told him he looked spicy hot
Neither of us knowing that in 36 hours he will physically stop
Equilibrium begin to drop
As reality started to mock
A visual thought
Where the color of reds
Worn to reflect what was ahead
Or was it a bud of a rose
Preparing to blossom I suppose
Into poetic prose
To the heavens above
Assisted by a dove
While surrounded by love

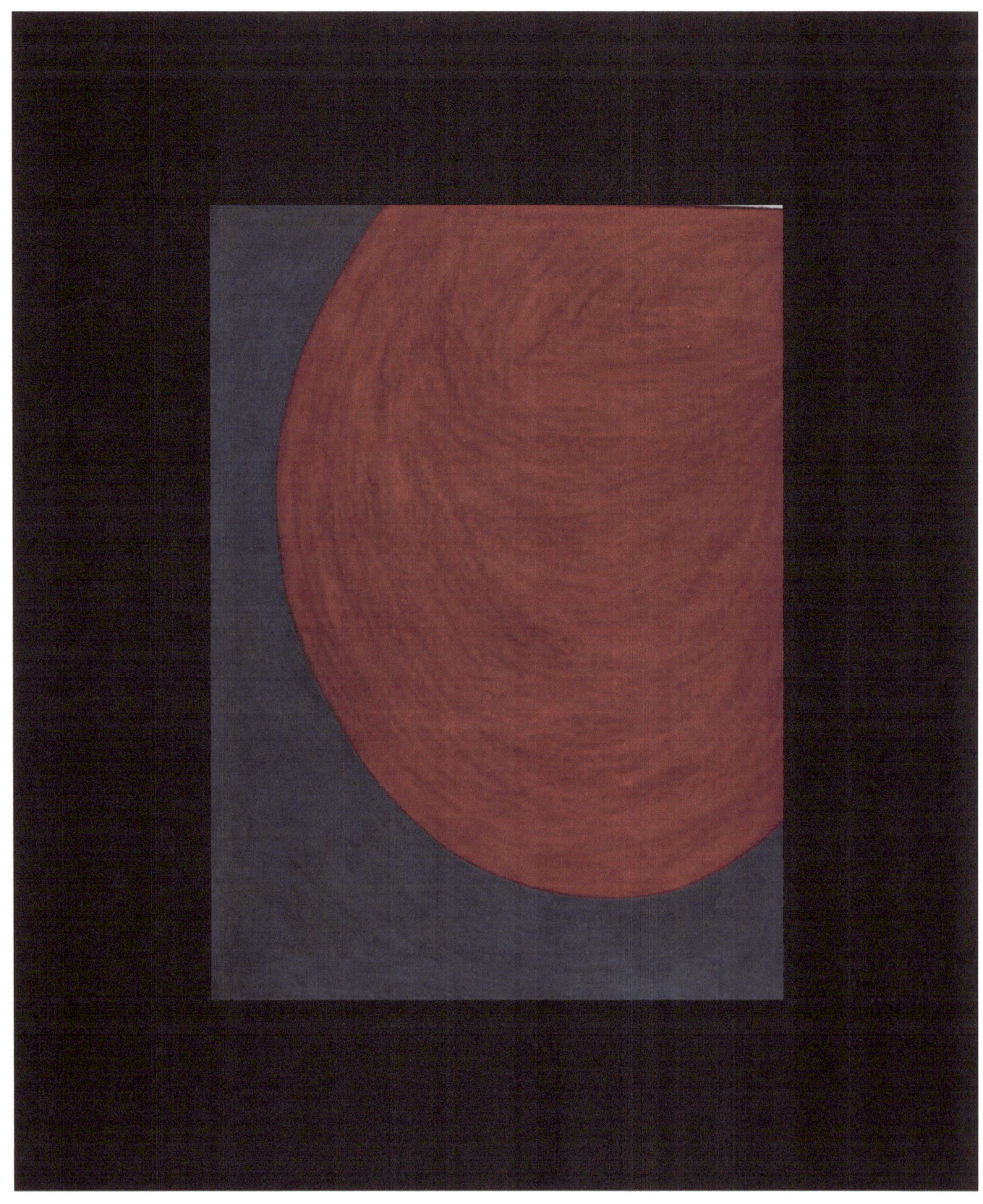

Focused Outlook

Focused Outlook

Have you ever had this feeling
Deep in the gut
As if you were not doing enough
It usually appears in spurts
Like when one pulls up
To a man holding a cup
Asking for change
In money and life
One turns away
Eyes focusing on the gray
Seated between the lights
Wondering when it might
Turn to green
Only when the eyes have truly seen
That were all connected in someway
Especially at times of dismay
Often projecting a hue
Seen by a few
When one is green
 Ignoring their dream
While chasing the cream
Of another's matured dream
Or a reflective yellow
With a demeanor that is mellow
Feet nestled around
What was found
To be their ground
And a few are ripe
Ready to bite

continued on next page

Just at the right moment in life
All as like grapes to a vine
Maturing with time
Clustered by type
While consuming sunlight
Fermented with care
Until one can share
The intoxicating gift
Baring the essence to uplift
Love

Focused Outlook

Carry On

Thrive

Thrive

There are many reasons to believe
And continue to achieve
In this journey of life
If not so, why are you reading this piece of write
It probably leads from the elevated height
Of knowing a challenge gives one the might
To adjust to a higher altitude of flight
By remembering to hold on tight
To the line of the kite
Seen mile upon mile
When a genuine smile
Allows inner child
To begin to stile
Accomplishments in a pile
Displayed proud
Without the cloud
Of conceit
Avoid this deceit
For their are lessons to learn
Before one may churn
The issues of life
Into the burn
Eliminating the yearn
While beginning to discern
Without concern
Toward a delight
That will unite

Stain Release

Stain Release

Ever been bit
By this thing that's no larger than a tick
See it likes to trick
One into believing their sick
Trying to prevent
The ability to vent
Even in the serenity of ones own tent
It comes in many forms
But loves to perform
Around in the head
Trying to knock talent dead
If this occurs
And the eyes begin to blur
Look at the clock
And begin to dock
The time one slid into writers block
This self- induced
Check of the mind
Will try to bind
Ones writing style
Use of words
Streams of confidence
Even accomplishments
Of some that have and have not been heard
This is not the norm
So do not mourn
Just try to remember a space
Where talent oozed from that place
Hands desperately trying to keep up with the pace
Pouring directly from the faucet leading from behind the face

continued on next page

Making a lasting memory with the assistance of a thin black or blue stained paste
With strokes of the hand gliding onto an empty bucket of waste
Ensuring quality and quantity without haste
By remaining true to the taste

Stain Release

/

Move Along

Authentic Strive

Authentic Strive

To stray from a talent
Is equivalent to being hit in the head with a mallet
The aftermath is the same
One looks for someone to blame
As one stumbles around
Often with a frown
Focused towards the ground
While floating upon the blue
Until one begins to
Humbly gather droplets of clear dew
Patiently forming into
Milky patches
Knowing no such things as latches
Driven by pure steam
Until manifested and projected from one as a beam
All the characteristics of a dream
Becoming surreal when one deeply believes
That nothing is a mistake
Just the opportunity to add another ingredient to life's cake
Which one can surely bake
With just the correct amount
Of ingredients leveled by consequences that sprout
From life lessons filing down self doubt
As the cake begins to form
One must decide which frosting is adorned

Renewed Purpose

Renewed Purpose

Fly
Forget about that thing called shy
Don't ask why
Just keep your head pointed towards the sky
My oh my
Even at times of cry
One must try
To move in a position
Once met with friction
But gives the prediction
That the road is smooth
Traveling toward what one is meant to do
While listening for the clue
When its one cue
So hang in there
Do not despair
It will only tear
From needed repair
But once this has passed
One will surly surpass
That transition as mere gas
While digesting the past
Into a cast
And uplifting the pace
Before one is laced
With the gift of grace

Amusement

Amusement

I have this dream
That there was no such thing
As putting someone down
And transferring the frown
No one prejudge
Because their hands were not part of the mud
Formed into clay
There is a better way
To calm the disarray
Only if one can be proud
Of the gift that allows
One not to cloud
Their silent loud
Incased
In a place
No one is able to erase
Seen for miles
When one displays a smile
Exposing the teeth
Lying directly beneath
The bow that propel positive or expel negative arrows be on belief
Giving many a warm feeling inside
Or tearing them apart
One must decide
Which attraction to ride

Poised Perception

Poised Perception

As like sandpaper is rough
Experience makes one tough
Depending upon the grit
Determines how and when the spark is lit
During these lessons in life
One is prepared for the strike
That will surly ignite
The flame within
Burning since one decided to lend
An ear to the voice
And begin to hoist
Option of choice
Across the tongue
Regardless of situation
Don't become tainted
With what the day has painted
To the canvas of life
Remain strong
Keep pushing on
While coming into own

Anchor

Anchor

How many in life
Will obtain a slice
Of something so nice
Weighing no more than a grain of rice
Enabling one to gain flight
After the patient hike
Composed of likes
And superficial spikes
Deflated by the one
That will balance the senses of love
Lying directly beneath and above
The communication hub
Ricocheting throughout the hull
While penetrating the skull
Slowly softening the inner shell
Allowing the scales that fell
To wash away
Day by day
Leaving a clear view
With a subtle hue
Of the glue
Used to mend
The heart again

Breathe

Breathe

Decompress
Allow the chest
To slowly move
With the hearts grove
Not required to prove
Ones worth
Come forth
In order to heal
One must patiently peel
Away the cast
Developed from the past
For some it's thick
If so, prepare to kick
Through the door
Leading to the core
Of the thrashing floor
Eliminating the rust
Formed on the crust
Into a dust
Resembling fresh powdered snow
A translucent glow
Flow

Direction

Direction

Poetry should be as warm to the soul
As prose describes a rose
Remaining simple
So it may ripple
A familiar tune
Once heard from the womb
Without the fume
To over consume
Providing harmony from the start
While caressing the heart
Thumping through the day
Pumping life into clay
Will begin to relay
Taking life too serious
Leaves one delirious
Often looking displaced
While becoming jaded from the space
That gave comfort from the mace
Of allowing one to paste
To the palates taste

Maintain

Maintain

What does one need
In order to feel free
To value ones life
Hurt know one out of spite
May it be on bended knee
With hands in the shape of a tee-pee
Gaining serenity
Or sitting on the edge
Obtaining vast amounts of disposable knowledge
Always remembering to pledge
To a cause that's lifeless and dead
For the sole purpose of the visual reflect on ones portfolio spread
Never quite sure where to lay thy head
Hoping peace will lye in the bed
Is it with one hand held tight
Around the sword that upholds the word
And the other slid through the bands of a shield
That has took one through many fields
Not preparing one to yield
But only to build
A glorious guild
Which we all can feel
From the bottom of thy heels
To overlooking a massive hill
All at ones own will
Fill

Release

Fly